101 Facts About

KITTENS

Published by Ringpress Books Limited,
PO Box 8, Lydney, Gloucestershire,
GL15 4YN, United Kingdom.

Design: Sara Howell

First Published 2001
© 2001 RINGPRESS BOOKS LIMITED

ISBN 1 86054 148 8

Printed in Hong Kong through Printworks Int. Ltd.

0 9 8 7 6 5 4 3 2 1

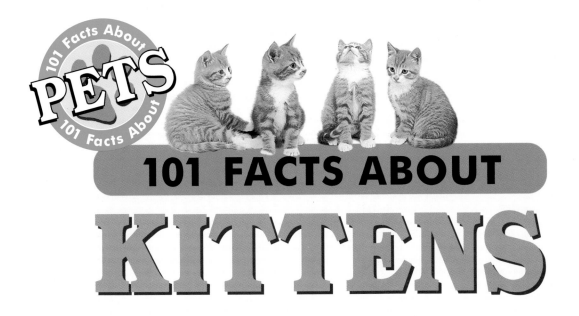

101 FACTS ABOUT

KITTENS

Claire Horton-Bussey

Ringpress Books

1 Have you ever seen a cat prowling in the undergrowth? He looks just like a miniature tiger. This is because the cats we keep as **pets** and the big cats (like lions and tigers) are closely related.

2 Pet cats are called **domestic cats**. They were tamed by humans about 4,000 years ago to keep rats and mice at bay.

3 Cats were worshipped by the Egyptians. They were considered special because they stopped rats and mice eating valuable grain that was made into bread. They also stopped the wild rats spreading diseases.

4 It is thought the word 'puss' comes from the Egyptian cat goddess Pasht.

5 Although domestic cats are much smaller than their wild cousins, they share many of the same characteristics. Although your kitten won't be able to hunt gazelle or other types of large prey, the hunting instinct is still very much alive.

6 Watch a kitten play with a toy. He will lower his head, flatten his body, and will concentrate on the 'prey'. Then he will wiggle his bottom slightly and pounce forward to 'kill' the toy.

7 Kittens start to play by about four weeks of age. They practise their hunting skills by creeping up on their mother and littermates.

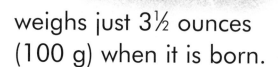

8 Of course, your kitten won't need to hunt to survive, as you will provide him with all the food he needs, but you can have lots of fun playing with toys.

9 You should spend time playing and cuddling your kitten every day to stop him from getting bored, and to help you build a close relationship together.

10 Kittens are born between 63 and 68 days after the parents have mated. The average kitten weighs just 3½ ounces (100 g) when it is born.

11 The size of a litter varies, but the average number of kittens is about six.

12 Kittens are born deaf. When they are four or five days old, they can hear some sounds, but it can be up to three months before their sensitive hearing is working properly.

15 Cats have very good vision to allow them to hunt, and they are also able to see in the dark. People used to think that cats only see in black and white, but scientists now think cats can see some colours.

13 Kittens are born blind, and their eyes will open after about a week. It will be three months before the kitten develops his sight fully.

16 Male kittens are called **tomcats** and females are called **queens**.

14 A kitten is born with blue eyes, but the eye colour usually changes to green as the kitten gets older. Some cats, such as Siamese, keep their blue eyes.

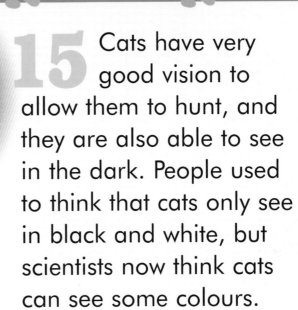

17 Cats are **carnivores**, meaning they need to eat meat to survive.

18 When he is first born, a kitten only needs his mother's milk. As he grows, a kitten needs solid food to give him the energy his growing body needs.

19 In preparation for solid food, kittens get their baby teeth at about three weeks of age.

20 When you first get your kitten he will probably need three or four small meals a day.

21 The number of meals can be reduced (and the amount increased) as the kitten grows, until, by the age of about seventeen weeks, he is enjoying just two meals each day.

22 Kittens do not drink a lot, but fresh water should always be available just in case he gets thirsty.

23 Many people think that cats should drink cow's milk, but this is not the case. Although most cats and kittens love milk, it is not always agreeable to them.

24 A kitten drinks – or 'laps' – by sticking his tongue out, dipping it into the drink, curling the end of it, and then flicking it into the back of his mouth to be swallowed.

25 When you first get your kitten home, you should take him to the vet to be checked over. The vet will tell you all about the **vaccinations** and other treatments your kitten may need.

26 Cats are very clean animals, and your kitten will start grooming himself at an early age.

27 Your kitten will groom using his rough tongue, and his flexible body will allow him to reach most of his body. Your kitten will lick his paw and then use it to wash the hard-to-reach places, such as behind his ears.

28 Grooming not only keeps the coat clean, but also separates the hairs to prevent knots and tangles from forming, especially in longhaired and semi-longhaired cats.

29 A well-groomed coat is essential to keep the cat warm in the winter and cool in the summer.

30 Although your kitten will groom himself, you should get him used to being brushed gently all over, too. Daily brushing will help to remove loose hair, and will prevent **furballs** from forming inside his tummy.

33 Kittens and **house-cats** will scratch against furniture or the carpet, but this will not wear down their claws, and they will probably need to have them clipped. A vet will do this for you.

31 Brush and comb your cat from head to tail, making sure you comb right down to the skin. Don't forget to comb your cat's tummy and under his arms.

32 Cats clean, sharpen, and wear down their claws by climbing and scratching against trees.

11

34 Kittens love special scratching posts where they can scratch to their hearts' content – without getting into trouble!

35 Cats have **retractable claws**, which means they can get their nails out when they are needed (such as when climbing), and tuck them away when they are not.

36 When you stroke your kitten on your lap, you may notice that he 'walks' on the spot, digging his front claws in your leg, before settling down to sleep. This is called '**milk-treading**' or 'kneading' and relates to when the kitten had to stimulate his mother's teat to get milk. If your kitten does it to you, it means he is very comfortable with you, and sees you as his mother-figure.

38 Kittens purr when they are feeding from their mother, when they are content, and even when they are in pain.

39 Kittens also purr when they are submissive – this means they want to show that they do not pose a threat.

37 When cuddling your kitten, you will hear him purring. It sounds just like a car engine gently revving. Domestic cats are the only animals that purr like this, and they start from when they are a week old.

40 Kittens make lots of other sounds. **Caterwauling** is a long howling noise that tomcats make when they are fighting over their territory.

13

41 Kittens can also growl. This is a low grumbling which is used as a warning, to tell another cat to go away.

42 Hissing and spitting is used when kittens are fighting. Your kitten will also bear his teeth when doing this, to make himself look more frightening and aggressive.

43 Kittens make lots of other sounds. There are many different types of miaow. Short or long, a miaow can mean many things – from 'hello' to 'feed me, please.'

44 Kittens like rubbing against things. This is so that they can mark their territory with their own scent.

45 Watch your kitten to see how **flexible** he is. He can twist and roll and get into all types of positions. This is because his bones are connected by muscles, which allow the body to stretch and bend.

46 Cats have 24 more bones than we do, and their skeleton is similar to a dog's.

47 You can learn a lot about your kitten by reading his body language.

48 When your kitten is happy, his tail will be high. A kitten about to hunt will hold his tail low, and a very scared cat will have his tail between his legs. A cat that is angry or worried will flick his tail.

50 Your kitten's eyes also give clues as to how he is feeling. When play-hunting, his eyes will widen and his pupils (the middle, black part of each eye) may get bigger.

49 A content kitten who feels confident and secure will have his ears forward. If he feels nervous or uncertain, the ears may go back to pick up sounds from all around. If your kitten is angry or ready to fight, the ears will flatten.

51 If threatened, your kitten will try to make himself look as large as possible, by arching his back and fluffing up his coat.

52 An angry cat may raise his 'hackles'. This means that the fur along his spine will stand on end.

53 The tail helps a kitten to balance, and helps him to walk across narrow paths without losing his footing. A tail is part of the kitten's spine, so should be handled very gently.

54 A kitten can cope without a tail, however. Some cats have their tails removed because they have been injured, and the **Manx cat** is a breed that never had a tail in the first place – it is born without one!

55 A kitten's whiskers are also important. They are very sensitive hairs that act like antennae (feelers) picking up vibrations. The kitten's eyebrows do the same.

56 Kittens have four rows of whiskers, which are usually longer than the cat is wide. This means that if a kitten's head and whiskers can pass through a gap, the body will fit, too.

57 When playing, a kitten's whiskers will move forward, to help him focus on his 'prey'.

58 A cat can sense if something is in front of him, even when he can't see. This is because his whiskers detect differences in air flow.

59 Sometimes, if a kitten is groomed too much by his mother, he can have his whiskers washed off! Luckily, the whiskers soon grow back.

60 Kittens are very clever and can be trained to do many things. One of the first things they will learn is their name. Say

your kitten's name as often as possible. Your kitten should associate his name with enjoyable things, such as being petted or being fed.

61 Your kitten will also need to learn to be toilet-trained. Kittens naturally look for somewhere to dig, so it won't take him long to be trained. Littertrays (literboxes) come in all shapes, colours and sizes. Your pet shop will have a variety to choose from.

62 Put the littertray in a quiet place where the kitten won't be disturbed. Fill it with about 2 inches (5 cms) of cat-litter. Put the kitten in, and encourage him to dig with his paws. Put the kitten in the tray regularly and he will soon start using the tray of his own accord.

63 Use a toy to teach your kitten simple tricks. Dangle a toy above his head, and when he sits back on his back legs to reach up to the toy, say "Up". Give him the toy as a reward. With practice, your kitten may learn to sit up just from you saying the command.

64 It is well known that dogs like playing fetch, but some kittens like the game too!

65 Throw a small toy for your kitten. His chase instinct will make the kitten run after the toy. As soon as he puts the toy in his mouth to 'kill' it, call him back to you. Hopefully, he will bring the toy with him.

66 You can also train your kitten to 'speak'. Whenever your kitten mews, say "Speak" and reward him with a cuddle.

67 You can also hold a treat in your hand and ask if he would like it. When he mews, give it to him. Be warned, though, once you teach a kitten to speak, it may be difficult to shut him up!

68 Some types of cat are more talkative than others. **Siamese** cats (above) are famous for being chatterboxes.

69 You can also train your kitten *not* to do things. If your kitten scratches the furniture instead of his scratching post, you should say "No!" firmly, and stop him at once.

70 There are **purebreed** cats (where both of the kitten's parents are a particular breed), and non-purebreed cats. **Crossbreed** cats are a mixture of two breeds.

71 There are also different coat types. Many cats are shorthaired, including the Siamese, British and American Shorthairs, and many non-purebreds.

72 Persians (above) and Chinchilla are purebred cats that have long coats, and they need regular grooming.

73 Some breeds, such as the Somali and Balinese, are semi-longhaired.

74 The Sphynx has just a few hairs, but they are not easy to spot!

75 Some cats have short, curly coats, such as the Devon Rex, and the Cornish Rex.

76 Ragdoll cats are so called because they are very laid-back, and tend to go limp like a ragdoll when picked up.

77 The Turkish Van comes from Lake Van in Turkey. The breed enjoys swimming and is fascinated by water. A Turkish Van kitten will spend hours playing with a running tap, dipping his paws in it.

78 Bengals also love water. Bengals have been created by crossing a domestic cat with an Asian leopard cat.

79 Kittens come in a range of different colours and shades – black, white, cream, ginger, brown, grey, silver, blue, lilac... the list is endless.

80 **Tortoiseshell** (above) is a mixture of black, red/orange and sometimes white. Most tortoiseshells are females (queens).

81 **Tabby** cats (right) come in red, silver, brown, chocolate and blue, and they can have a variety of markings – stripy, marbled, spotted or ticked (where each individual hair has different bands of colour).

82 'Colourpoint' means the body is a lighter colour than the head and other extreme points – such as the bottom of the legs and the tail. Colourpoint Siamese and Ragdolls have this type of marking.

83 Your kitten should have his own place to sleep. Many like beds

that are covered with hoods, as they are warm and draught-free. Sleeping-bag type beds are also popular as kittens can tunnel into them.

84 Kittens need lots of cat-naps throughout the day to recover from all the playing and growing they do. Your kitten's bed should be placed somewhere quiet, where he won't be disturbed.

85 Your cat should have a collar with your telephone number on, so if he gets lost, he can be returned to you. The collar should be safe so that if your kitten gets it caught on something, he will be able to get free. Some collars unclip or stretch when they get caught.

86 Collars with bells will stop your cat from killing any birds or mice, as they will hear him coming! There are even electronic collars which warn birds when the cat is about to pounce.

87 Your kitten should also have a good selection of strong, safe toys. Balls and dangle toys (like fishing rods) are very popular.

88 **Catnip** is a safe herb which drives some kittens crazy. Others aren't affected by it at all.

89 If your kitten gets a little bored with one of his toys, sprinkle on some catnip powder. If he rolls around and acts a little beserk, it means he likes it!

90 Your kitten shouldn't be allowed outside until he has had his vaccinations to keep him safe against serious diseases.

91 Once he is allowed out, take him to your garden and let him investigate for a while. Eventually, you can fit a cat flap to your door so he can come and go as he wishes.

92 Many cats are killed on busy roads each year, and some people decide never to let their kittens outside, preferring to keep them as **house-cats**.

93 House-cats should be given lots of opportunities for climbing and playing. They should also be given indoor grass, (from pet stores), which is grown in small containers.

94 Kittens need to eat grass to help their digestion. It also helps them to get rid of **furballs**.

95 Make sure your kitten can't chew any house-plants, as some (such as ivy and spider plants) are poisonous. Keep all plants safely out of reach.

96 Your kitten's curiosity can also get him into trouble. If a wardrobe door is open, your kitten will shoot in to explore. If the tumbledryer door is ajar, your kitten will crawl in and curl up to sleep.

97 Always keep an eye on your kitten, and when you are not able to, keep him safely shut in a kitten-safe room.

98 Kittens are fairly tough, despite their size, and this is where the belief that a "cat has nine lives" comes from.

99 Of course, a cat only has one life – and most live to around 14 years of age.

100 Some cats live way beyond this, though. Puss, a tabby from Devon, England, died a day after his 36th birthday, back in 1939.

101 Kittens are incredibly cute, but grow up so quickly. The good news is that when they are fully grown, they are just as wonderful, and you will continue to have great fun together for many years to come.

GLOSSARY

Carnivore: something that eats meat.

Caterwauling: long howling noise that tomcats make when they are fighting.

Catnip: a herb which drives some cats wild!

Colourpoint: where the cat's body is a lighter colour than the head, legs and tail.

Crossbreed: a cat that is a mixture of two breeds.

Domestic cat: a tame pet cat.

Flexible: able to move, bend and twist easily in lots of different positions.

Furball: a clump of swallowed fur.

House-cat: a cat that is kept indoors, and is not let outside.

Mats: knots and tangles in the fur.

Milk-treading: where the cat walks on the spot, kneading his bed or his owner's lap.

Purebreed: a kitten whose parents are the same breed.

Queen: a female cat.

Retractable claws: claws that can be drawn back and tucked safely away.

Tabby: a red, silver, brown, chocolate or blue coat, that has stripy, marbled, spotted or ticked markings.

Ticked: where each individual hair has different bands of colour.

Tomcat: a male cat.

Tortoiseshell: a coat that is a mixture of black, red/orange and sometimes white.

Vaccinations: injections which protect your kitten against serious diseases.

MORE BOOKS TO READ

All About Your Kitten
Bradley Viner
(Ringpress Books)

Pet Owner's Guide to Kitten Care and Training
Andrea McHugh
(Ringpress Books)

All About Cats and Kittens
Emily Neye
(Grosset & Dunlap)

How to Talk to Your Cat
Jean Craighead George
(HarperCollins Juvenile Books)

 # WEBSITES

Kitten care
www.kittencare.com

Kitty-cats
www.kitty-cats.com

Thinking of adopting a cat?
prince.thinkquest.org/4213/

Very best pet
www.verybestpet.com

To find additional websites, use a reliable search engine to find one or more of the following key words: **kitten, kitten care, cats.**

INDEX